1 dough, 50 cookies

Linda Doeser

This edition published 2012 for Index Books Ltd
LOVE FOOD is an imprint of Parragon Books Ltd

Parragon
Queen Street House
4 Queen Street
Bath BA1 1HE, UK

ISBN: 978-1-78186-200-1

Printed in China

Written by Linda Doeser
Internal design by Simon Levy
Photography by Clive Streeter
Home economy by Angela Drake, Teresa Goldfinch and Carole
Streeter

Notes for the Reader
This book uses both metric and imperial measurements. Follow
the same units of measurement throughout; do not mix metric and
imperial. All spoon measurements are level: teaspoons are assumed
to be 5 ml, and tablespoons are assumed to be 15 ml. Unless
otherwise stated, milk is assumed to be full-fat, eggs and individual
vegetables are medium, and pepper is freshly ground black pepper.

The times given are an approximate guide only. Preparation times
differ according to the techniques used by different people, and the
cooking times may also vary from those given. Optional ingredients,
variations or serving suggestions have not been included in the
calculations.

Recipes using raw or very lightly cooked eggs should be avoided
by infants, the elderly, pregnant women, convalescents and anyone
suffering from an illness. Pregnant and breastfeeding women are
advised to avoid eating peanuts and peanut products. Sufferers
from nut allergies should be aware that some of the ready-made
ingredients used in the recipes in this book may contain nuts.
Always check the packaging before use.

Contents

Introduction

Whether we're desperate for a well-earned mid-morning cup of coffee or the kids have come home from school too ravenous to wait until supper time, cookies will invariably hit the spot. Sometimes, we just want to congratulate ourselves with a little self-indulgent treat; at others we require a subtle accompaniment to a spectacular dinner party dessert. Equally, we might want to make a colourful, fun snack for a child's birthday or to bake edible decorations for the Christmas tree.

The great thing about home-made cookies – apart from the fact that they taste terrific – is that they are quick and easy to make and astonishingly versatile. There are recipes for fifty different cookies in this book, ranging from wonderfully sticky and rich chocolate treats to crisp and crunchy snacks, and from positively sinful nibbles with cocktail-flavoured icing to fruit-and-nut filled delights. The beauty of this book is that every single recipe is based on the Basic Cookie Dough (see page 8). All you need to do is add a few variations, how simple is that!

Equipment

You won't need to buy any expensive or specialist kitchen tools. In fact, you probably already have most of what's required – scales, measuring spoons, mixing bowls, wooden spoons, chopping knives, whisks, palette knife, rolling pin and a sieve.

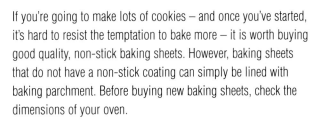

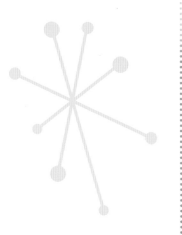

If you're going to make lots of cookies – and once you've started, it's hard to resist the temptation to bake more – it is worth buying good quality, non-stick baking sheets. However, baking sheets that do not have a non-stick coating can simply be lined with baking parchment. Before buying new baking sheets, check the dimensions of your oven.

Baking parchment, which has a shiny, non-stick surface, is useful in a number of ways. When rolling out cookie dough, it's better to put the dough between two sheets of baking parchment than to dust the work surface with flour. This is because even a little flour can affect the texture and appearance of the cookies. Some decorated cookies and crystallized flowers and fruit are best left to dry on a sheet of baking parchment.

One or more wire racks is essential when the cookies are cooling, as the design allows air to circulate, thus preventing the cookies from becoming soggy. They are available in different shapes and sizes.

It is quite likely that you already have cookie cutters but there is such a range of shapes and sizes that you might be tempted to buy some more, particularly for festive cookies or special occasions. Some of the cutters available include plain and fluted rounds, hearts, stars, crescents, snowflakes, numbers, alphabet, squares, rectangles, holly leaves, Christmas trees and even Father Christmas – not to mention gingerbread and teddy bear families. Metal cutters are better than plastic, as they don't compress the edges of the cookies.

You will find that there are many ways to ice and decorate cookies without needing an icing bag. However, a medium-sized bag, preferably double-stitched for strength, and a selection of nozzles won't break the bank and might inspire your creative instincts. As the decoration on cookies is less elaborate than on cakes, a small plastic bag with the corner snipped off is often all that's required.

Ingredients

Butter is the ideal fat for making cookies, giving them a rich flavour that margarine can't match. Unsalted butter is best for sweet baking. The recipes in this book involve creaming the butter with the sugar, so remove the butter from the refrigerator in advance to allow time for it to soften slightly. Caster sugar is the type most frequently used for making cookies because the grains are very fine and it combines easily with the other ingredients. It is also used for sprinkling over freshly baked cookies. Some recipes specify golden caster sugar, which has exactly the same qualities as white sugar but provides extra colour. Caster sugar may be flavoured in a variety of ways. The most common method is to put a vanilla pod in a jar of sugar and leave it for about a week. An unusual and aromatic flavour is produced by putting rose petals in a jar of sugar. Make sure that they are fresh, dry, disease-free and have not been sprayed with chemicals.

Icing sugar is powdery and used to make icings and buttercream fillings. It can also be dusted over cookies to decorate. It should always be sifted first.

Coffee, demerara and granulated sugars may all be used to decorate cookies.

The flour used in the Basic Cookie Dough in this book is plain flour and it should be sifted even if it is labelled ready-sifted.

Egg yolk is used to bind the dry ingredients together and it also helps to enrich the dough. Remove eggs from the refrigerator in advance to allow them to come to room temperature. You can use an egg separator to separate the yolk from the white or just tip the whole egg into your hand and allow the white to drain through your fingers. A less messy way is to crack the shell and prise it apart, then allow the white to drain into a bowl while retaining the yolk in a half shell. Tip the yolk into the other half shell to allow the remaining white to drain.

Various aromatic extracts are available, the most commonly used being vanilla, which goes well with lots of other flavours including chocolate. Others used in this book include almond, orange and peppermint. When buying, check the labels carefully to avoid artificial flavourings.

A huge range of dried fruits is available nowadays from classic vine fruits, such as currants, to exotic varieties, such as papaya. Both dried and crystallized fruits are great for flavouring cookies.

Nuts are a popular flavouring and also add texture to cookies. They may be used whole, chopped or ground and can feature as decoration as well as forming part of the dough. Nuts cannot be stored for very long, so buy them in small quantities and keep in an airtight container.

Plain, dark, milk and white chocolate feature in both cookie dough and cookie decorations, whether chopped, grated, melted or in the form of chocolate chips or chocolate vermicelli. Good quality, sifted cocoa powder also adds a rich chocolate flavour to the dough and can be dusted over baked cookies.

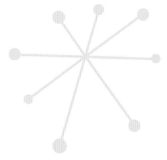

Basic Cookie Dough

Makes about 30

* 225 g/8 oz butter, softened
* 140 g/5 oz caster sugar
* 1 egg yolk, lightly beaten
* 2 tsp vanilla extract
* 280 g/10 oz plain flour
* salt

This is the recipe that all 50 variations of cookie in the book are based on.

For each recipe the basic mix is highlighted (*) for easy reference, so then all you have to do is follow the easy steps each time and a world of delicious and delectable cookies will await you.

Please note the basic ingredients may vary from time to time so please check these carefully.

Gooey

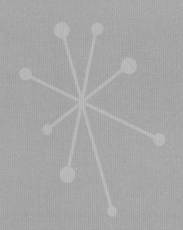

Mega Chip Cookies

1. Preheat the oven to 190°C/375°F/Gas Mark 5. Line 2–3 baking sheets with baking parchment.

2. Put the butter and sugar into a bowl and mix well with a wooden spoon, then beat in the egg yolk and vanilla extract. Sift together the flour, cocoa powder and a pinch of salt into the mixture, add both kinds of chocolate chips and stir until thoroughly combined.

3. Make 12 balls of the mixture, put them on to the prepared baking sheets, spaced well apart, and flatten slightly. Press the pieces of dark chocolate into the cookies.

4. Bake for 12–15 minutes. Leave to cool on the baking sheets for 5–10 minutes, then using a palette knife, carefully transfer to wire racks to cool completely.

Makes 12 large cookies

* 225 g/8 oz butter, softened
* 140 g/5 oz caster sugar
* 1 egg yolk, lightly beaten
* 2 tsp vanilla extract
* 225 g/8 oz plain flour
  55 g/2 oz cocoa powder
  85 g/3 oz milk chocolate chips
  85 g/3 oz white chocolate chips
  115 g/4 oz dark chocolate, coarsely chopped
* salt

2

Almond & Raspberry Jam Drops

1. Preheat the oven to 190°C/375°F/Gas Mark 5. Line 2 baking sheets with baking parchment.

2. Put the butter and sugar into a bowl and mix well with a wooden spoon, then beat in the egg yolk and almond extract. Sift together the flour and a pinch of salt into the mixture, add the almonds and mixed peel and stir until thoroughly combined.

3. Scoop out tablespoons of the mixture and shape into balls with your hands, then put them on to the prepared baking sheets, spaced well apart. Use the dampened handle of a wooden spoon to make a hollow in the centre of each cookie and fill the hollows with raspberry jam.

4. Bake for 12–15 minutes, until golden brown. Leave to cool on the baking sheets for 5–10 minutes, then using a palette knife, carefully transfer the cookies to wire racks to cool completely.

Makes about 25

※ 225 g/8 oz butter, softened
※ 140 g/5 oz caster sugar
※ 1 egg yolk, lightly beaten
2 tsp almond extract
※ 280 g/10 oz plain flour
55 g/2 oz almonds, toasted and chopped
55 g/2 oz chopped mixed peel
4 tbsp raspberry jam
※ salt

Orange & Chocolate Fingers

1. Put the butter, sugar and orange rind into a bowl and mix well with a wooden spoon, then beat in the egg yolk and orange juice. Sift together the flour, ginger and a pinch of salt into the mixture and stir until thoroughly combined. Shape the dough into a ball, wrap in clingfilm and chill in the refrigerator for 30–60 minutes.

2. Preheat the oven to 190°C/375°F/Gas Mark 5. Line 2 baking sheets with baking parchment.

3. Unwrap the dough and roll out between 2 sheets of baking parchment to a rectangle. Using a sharp knife, cut it into 10 x 2-cm/4 x ¾-inch strips and put them on the prepared baking sheets spaced well apart.

4. Bake for 10–12 minutes, until light golden brown. Leave to cool on the baking sheets for 5–10 minutes, then using a palette knife, carefully transfer to wire racks to cool completely.

5. Put the pieces of chocolate into a heatproof bowl and melt over a pan of gently simmering water, then remove from the heat and leave to cool. When the chocolate is cool but not set, dip the cookies diagonally into it to half coat, then put on the wire racks and leave to set. You may find it easier to do this using tongs.

Makes about 35

* 225 g/8 oz butter, softened
* 140 g/5 oz caster sugar
   grated rind of 1 orange
* 1 egg yolk, lightly beaten
   2 tsp orange juice
* 280 g/10 oz plain flour
   1 tsp ground ginger
   115 g/4 oz dark chocolate, broken into pieces
* salt

Pear & Mint Cookies

1. Put the butter and sugar into a bowl and mix well with a wooden spoon, then beat in the egg yolk and vanilla extract. Sift together the flour and a pinch of salt into the mixture, add the pears and stir until thoroughly combined. Shape the mixture into a log, wrap in clingfilm and chill in the refrigerator for 30–60 minutes.

2. Preheat the oven to 190°C/375°F/Gas Mark 5. Line 2 baking sheets with baking parchment.

3. Unwrap the log and cut it into 5-mm/¼-inch slices with a sharp serrated knife. Put them on to the prepared baking sheets spaced well apart.

4. Bake for 10–15 minutes, until golden brown. Leave to cool on the baking sheets for 5–10 minutes, then using a palette knife, carefully transfer the cookies to wire racks to cool completely.

5. To decorate, sift the icing sugar into a bowl and stir in the peppermint extract. Gradually stir in the hot water until the icing has the consistency of double cream. Leave the cooled cookies on the wire racks and drizzle lines of icing over them, using a teaspoon. Leave to set.

Makes about 30

* 225 g/8 oz butter, softened
* 140 g/5 oz caster sugar
* 1 egg yolk, lightly beaten
* 2 tsp vanilla extract
* 280 g/10 oz plain flour
  100 g/3½ oz dried pears, finely chopped
* salt

To decorate
115 g/4 oz icing sugar
few drops of peppermint extract
1 tbsp hot water

5

Chocolate, Date & Pecan Nut Pinwheels

1. Put the butter and 140 g/5 oz of the sugar into a bowl and mix well with a wooden spoon, then beat in the egg yolk. Sift together the flour, cocoa powder and a pinch of salt into the mixture, add the pecan nuts and stir until thoroughly combined. Halve the dough, shape into balls, wrap in clingfilm and chill for 30–60 minutes.

2. Meanwhile, put the dried dates, orange rind, orange flower water and remaining sugar into a saucepan and cook over a low heat, stirring constantly, until the sugar has dissolved. Bring to the boil, then lower the heat and simmer, stirring occasionally, for 5 minutes. Remove the pan from the heat, pour the mixture into a bowl and leave to cool, then chill in the refrigerator.

3. Unwrap the dough and roll out between 2 pieces of baking parchment to rectangles about 5 mm/¼ inch thick. Spread the date filling evenly over the rectangles. Roll up the dough from a short side like a Swiss roll, wrap in the baking parchment and chill for a further 30 minutes.

4. Preheat the oven to 190°C/375°F/Gas Mark 5. Line 2 baking sheets with baking parchment.

5. Unwrap the rolls and cut into 1-cm/½-inch slices. Put them on the prepared baking sheets and bake for 15–20 minutes, until golden brown. Leave to cool on the baking sheets for 5–10 minutes, then carefully transfer to wire racks to cool completely.

Makes about 30

* 225 g/8 oz butter, softened
* 200 g/7 oz caster sugar
* 1 egg yolk, lightly beaten
* 225 g/8 oz plain flour
  55 g/2 oz cocoa powder
  100 g/3½ oz pecan nuts, finely ground
  280 g/10 oz dried dates, coarsely chopped
  finely grated rind of 1 orange
  175 ml/6 fl oz orange flower water
* salt

Marshmallow Daisies

1. Put the butter and sugar into a bowl and mix well with a wooden spoon, then beat in the egg yolk and vanilla extract. Sift together the flour, cocoa powder and a pinch of salt into the mixture and stir until thoroughly combined. Halve the dough, roll each piece into a ball, wrap in clingfilm and chill in the refrigerator for 30–60 minutes.

2. Preheat the oven to 190°C/375°F/Gas Mark 5. Line 2 baking sheets with baking parchment.

3. Unwrap the dough and roll out between 2 sheets of baking parchment to about 1 cm/½ inch thick and stamp out about 30 cookies with a 5-cm/2-inch flower cutter. Put them on the prepared baking sheets spaced well apart.

4. Bake for 10–12 minutes, until firm. Remove the baking sheets from the oven but do not turn off the heat. Arrange the pieces of marshmallow over the petals of the flowers, cutting them to fit if necessary. Return to the oven for 30–60 seconds, until the marshmallow has softened.

5. Leave to cool on the baking sheets for 5–10 minutes, then using a palette knife, carefully transfer the cookies to wire racks to cool completely. Meanwhile, heat the jam in a small saucepan, strain into a bowl and leave to cool. Pipe a small circle of jam in the centre of each flower and top with the sugar sprinkles.

- 225 g/8 oz butter, softened
- 140 g/5 oz caster sugar
- 1 egg yolk, lightly beaten
- 2 tsp vanilla extract
- 225 g/8 oz plain flour
- 55 g/2 oz cocoa powder
- about 90 white mini marshmallows, halved horizontally
- 4 tbsp peach jam
- 4 tbsp yellow sugar sprinkles
- salt

23

7

Peanut Partners

1. Put the butter and sugar into a bowl and mix well with a wooden spoon, then beat in the egg yolk. Sift together the flour, ginger and a pinch of salt into the mixture, add the lemon rind and stir until thoroughly combined. Halve the dough, shape into balls, wrap in clingfilm and chill in the refrigerator for 30–60 minutes.

2. Preheat the oven to 190°C/375°F/Gas Mark 5. Line 2 baking sheets with baking parchment.

3. Unwrap the dough and roll out between 2 sheets of baking parchment to about 3 mm/⅛ inch thick. Stamp out rounds with a 6-cm/2½-inch fluted cutter and put them on the prepared baking sheets spaced well apart.

4. Bake for 10–15 minutes, until golden brown. Leave to cool on the baking sheets for 5–10 minutes, then using a palette knife, carefully transfer the cookies to wire racks to cool completely.

5. Beat together the peanut butter and icing sugar in a bowl, adding a little water if necessary. Spread the cookies with the peanut butter mixture and decorate with whole or chopped peanuts.

Makes about 30

* 225 g/8 oz butter, softened
* 140 g/5 oz caster sugar
* 1 egg yolk, lightly beaten
* 280 g/10 oz plain flour
   1 tsp ground ginger
   2 tsp finely grated lemon rind
   3 tbsp smooth peanut butter
   3 tbsp icing sugar
* salt
   whole or chopped roasted peanuts, to decorate

Chocolate Sprinkle Cookies

1. Put the butter and sugar into a bowl and mix well with a wooden spoon, then beat in the egg yolk and vanilla extract. Sift together the flour, cocoa powder and a pinch of salt into the mixture and stir until thoroughly combined. Halve the dough, roll each piece into a ball, wrap in clingfilm and chill in the refrigerator for 30–60 minutes to firm up.

2. Preheat the oven to 190°C/375°F/Gas Mark 5. Line 2 baking sheets with baking parchment.

3. Unwrap the dough and roll out between 2 pieces of baking parchment to about 5 mm/¼ inch thick and stamp out 30 cookies with a 6–7-cm/2½–2¾-inch fluted round cutter. Put them on the prepared baking sheets spaced well apart.

4. Bake for 10–12 minutes. Leave to cool on the baking sheets for 5–10 minutes, then using a palette knife, carefully transfer the cookies to wire racks to cool completely.

5. Put the pieces of white chocolate into a heatproof bowl and melt over a pan of gently simmering water, then immediately remove from the heat. Spread the melted chocolate over the cookies, leave to cool slightly and then sprinkle with the chocolate vermicelli. Leave to cool and set.

Makes about 30

- 225 g/8 oz butter, softened
- 140 g/5 oz caster sugar
- 1 egg yolk, lightly beaten
- 2 tsp vanilla extract
- 225 g/8 oz plain flour, plus extra for dusting
- 55 g/2 oz cocoa powder
- 200 g/7 oz white chocolate, broken into pieces
- 85 g/3 oz chocolate vermicelli
- salt

Treacle & Spice Drizzles

1. Put the butter, treacle and sugar into a bowl and mix well with a wooden spoon, then beat in the egg yolk. Sift together the flour, cinnamon, nutmeg, cloves and a pinch of salt into the mixture, add the walnuts and stir until thoroughly combined. Halve the dough, shape into balls, wrap in clingfilm and chill in the refrigerator for 30–60 minutes.

2. Preheat the oven to 190°C/375°F/Gas Mark 5. Line 2 baking sheets with baking parchment.

3. Unwrap the dough and roll out between 2 sheets of baking parchment to about 5 mm/¼ inch thick. Stamp out rounds with a 6-cm/2½-inch fluted cutter and put them on the prepared baking sheets.

4. Bake for 10–15 minutes, until firm. Leave to cool on the baking sheets for 5–10 minutes, then using a palette knife, carefully transfer the cookies to wire racks to cool completely.

5. For the icing, sift the icing sugar into a bowl, then gradually stir in the hot water until the icing has the consistency of thick cream. Spoon half the icing into another bowl and stir a few drops of yellow food colouring into one bowl and a few drops of pink food colouring into the other. Leave the cookies on the racks and, using teaspoons, drizzle the yellow icing over them in one direction and the pink icing over them at right angles. Leave to set.

Makes about 25

✳ 200 g/7 oz butter, softened
2 tbsp black treacle
✳ 140 g/5 oz caster sugar
✳ 1 egg yolk, lightly beaten
✳ 280 g/10 oz plain flour
1 tsp ground cinnamon
½ tsp grated nutmeg
½ tsp ground cloves
2 tbsp chopped walnuts
✳ salt

Icing
115 g/4 oz icing sugar
1 tbsp hot water
a few drops of yellow food colouring
a few drops of pink food colouring

Chocolate Spread & Hazelnut Drops

1. Preheat the oven to 190°C/375°F/Gas Mark 5. Line 2 baking sheets with baking parchment.

2. Put the butter and sugar into a bowl and mix well with a wooden spoon, then beat in the egg yolk and vanilla extract. Sift together the flour, cocoa and a pinch of salt into the mixture, add the ground hazelnuts and stir until thoroughly combined.

3. Scoop out tablespoons of the mixture and shape into balls with your hands, then put them on to the prepared baking sheets spaced well apart. Use the dampened handle of a wooden spoon to make a hollow in the centre of each cookie.

4. Bake for 12–15 minutes. Leave to cool on the baking sheets for 5–10 minutes, then using a palette knife, carefully transfer the cookies to wire racks to cool completely. When they are cold, fill the hollows in the centre with chocolate and hazelnut spread.

Makes about 30

- 225 g/8 oz butter, softened
- 140 g/5 oz caster sugar
- 1 egg yolk, lightly beaten
- 2 tsp vanilla extract
- 225 g/8 oz plain flour
- 55 g/2 oz cocoa powder
- 55 g/2 oz ground hazelnuts
- 55 g/2 oz plain chocolate chips
- 4 tbsp chocolate and hazelnut spread
- salt

Crunch

Almond Crunchies

1. Put the butter and sugar into a bowl and mix well with a wooden spoon, then beat in the egg yolk and almond extract. Sift together the flour and a pinch of salt into the mixture, add the almonds and stir until thoroughly combined. Halve the dough, shape it into balls, wrap in clingfilm and chill in the refrigerator for 30–60 minutes.

2. Preheat the oven to 190°C/375°F/Gas Mark 5. Line 2–3 baking sheets with baking parchment.

3. Shape the dough into about 50 small balls and flatten them slightly between the palms of your hands. Put on the prepared baking sheets spaced well apart.

4. Bake for 15–20 minutes, until golden brown. Leave to cool on the baking sheets for 5–10 minutes, then using a palette knife, carefully transfer to wire racks to cool completely.

Makes about 50

* 225 g/8 oz butter, softened
* 140 g/5 oz caster sugar
* 1 egg yolk, lightly beaten
  ½ tsp almond extract
* 225 g/8 oz plain flour
  225 g/8 oz blanched almonds, chopped
* salt

Flower Gems

1. Put the butter and sugar into a bowl and mix well with a wooden spoon, then beat in the egg yolk and lemon juice. Sift together the flour and a pinch of salt into the mixture, add the tea leaves and stir until thoroughly combined. Halve the dough, shape it into balls, wrap in clingfilm and chill in the refrigerator for 30–60 minutes.

2. Preheat the oven to 190°C/375°F/Gas Mark 5. Line 2 baking sheets with baking parchment.

3. Roll out the dough between 2 sheets of baking parchment to about 3 mm/⅛ inch thick. Stamp out flowers with a 5-cm/2-inch flower cutter. Put them on the prepared baking sheets spaced well apart.

4. Bake for 10–12 minutes, until golden brown. Leave to cool on the baking sheets for 5–10 minutes, then carefully transfer the cookies to wire racks to cool completely.

5. To decorate, mix the lemon juice with 1 tbsp water in a bowl, then gradually stir in enough icing sugar to make a mixture with the consistency of thick cream. Divide the icing among 4 separate bowls and add a drop of different food colouring to each.

6. Leave the cookies on the racks. Spread orange icing on a quarter of the cookies, pink on another quarter and so on. When the icing is beginning to set, add a matching flower in the centre of each. Leave to cool.

Makes about 30

- 225 g/8 oz butter, softened
- 140 g/5 oz caster sugar
- 1 egg yolk, lightly beaten
- 1 tsp lemon juice
- 280 g/10 oz plain flour
- 2 tbsp jasmine tea leaves
- salt

To decorate
1 tbsp lemon juice
200 g/7 oz icing sugar
orange, pink, blue and yellow food colouring
orange, pink, blue and yellow sugar flowers

Rose Flower Cookies

1. Put the butter and sugar into a bowl and mix well with a wooden spoon, then beat in the egg and rose water. Sift together the flour, baking powder and a pinch of salt into the mixture and stir until thoroughly combined. Shape the dough into a log, wrap in clingfilm and chill in the refrigerator for 1–2 hours.

2. Preheat the oven to 190°C/375°F/Gas Mark 5. Line 2–3 baking sheets with baking parchment.

3. Unwrap the dough and cut into thin slices with a sharp serrated knife. Put on the prepared baking sheets spaced well apart. Bake for 10–12 minutes, until light golden brown. Leave the cookies to cool on the baking sheets for 10 minutes, then using a palette knife, carefully transfer them to wire racks to cool completely.

4. To make the icing, lightly beat the egg white with a fork in a bowl. Sift in half the icing sugar and stir well, then sift in the remaining icing sugar and flour and mix in sufficient rose water to make a smooth, easy-to-spread icing. Stir in a few drops of pink food colouring.

5. Leave the cookies on the racks. Gently spread the icing over them and leave to set.

Makes about 55–60

- 225 g/8 oz butter, softened
- 225 g/8 oz caster sugar
- 1 large egg, lightly beaten
- 1 tbsp rose water
- 280 g/10 oz plain flour
- 1 tsp baking powder
- salt

Icing
- 1 egg white
- 250 g/9 oz icing sugar
- 2 tsp plain flour
- 2 tsp rose water
- pink food colouring

Cashew & Poppy Seed Cookies

1. Put the butter and sugar into a bowl and mix well with a wooden spoon, then beat in the egg yolk. Sift together the flour, cinnamon and a pinch of salt into the mixture, add the nuts and stir until thoroughly combined. Shape the dough into a log. Spread out the poppy seeds in a shallow dish and roll the log in them until well coated. Wrap in clingfilm and chill in the refrigerator for 30–60 minutes.

2. Preheat the oven to 190°C/375°F/Gas Mark 5. Line 2 baking sheets with baking parchment.

3. Unwrap the dough and cut into 1-cm/½-inch slices with a sharp serrated knife. Put them on the prepared baking sheets and bake for 12 minutes, until golden brown. Leave to cool on the baking sheets for 5–10 minutes, then using a palette knife, carefully transfer to wire racks to cool completely.

Makes about 20

* 225 g/8 oz butter, softened
* 140 g/5 oz caster sugar
* 1 egg yolk, lightly beaten
* 280 g/10 oz plain flour
  1 tsp ground cinnamon
  115 g/4 oz cashew nuts, chopped
  2–3 tbsp poppy seeds
* salt

15

Biscotti

1. Put the butter, sugar and lemon rind into a bowl and mix well with a wooden spoon, then beat in the egg yolk and brandy. Sift together the flour and a pinch of salt into the mixture, add the pistachio nuts and stir until thoroughly combined. Shape the mixture into a log, flatten slightly, wrap in clingfilm and chill in the refrigerator for 30–60 minutes.

2. Preheat the oven to 190°C/375°F/Gas Mark 5. Line 2 baking sheets with baking parchment.

3. Unwrap the log and cut it slightly on the diagonal into 5-mm/¼-inch slices with a sharp serrated knife. Put them on the prepared baking sheets spaced well apart.

4. Bake for 10 minutes, until golden brown. Leave to cool on the baking sheets for 5–10 minutes, then using a palette knife, carefully transfer to wire racks to cool completely. Dust with icing sugar.

Makes about 30

* 225 g/8 oz butter, softened
* 140 g/5 oz caster sugar
  finely grated rind of 1 lemon
* 1 egg yolk, lightly beaten
  2 tsp brandy
* 280 g/10 oz plain flour
  85 g/3 oz pistachio nuts
* salt
  icing sugar, for dusting

Golden Hazelnut Cookies

1. Put the butter and sugar into a bowl and mix well with a wooden spoon, then beat in the egg yolk. Sift together the flour and a pinch of salt into the mixture, add the ground hazelnuts and stir until thoroughly combined. Halve the dough, form into balls, wrap in clingfilm and chill in the refrigerator for 30–60 minutes.

2. Preheat the oven to 190°C/375°F/Gas Mark 5. Line 2 baking sheets with baking parchment.

3. Unwrap the dough and roll out between 2 sheets of baking parchment. Stamp out rounds with a plain 6-cm/2½-inch cutter and put them on the prepared baking sheets spaced well apart.

4. Bake for 10–12 minutes, until golden brown. Leave to cool for 5–10 minutes, then carefully transfer the cookies to wire racks to cool.

5. When the cookies are cool, place the wire racks over a sheet of baking parchment. Put the chocolate into a heatproof bowl and melt over a pan of gently simmering water. Remove the bowl from the heat and leave to cool, then spoon the chocolate over the cookies. Gently tap the wire racks to level the surface.

6. Add a hazelnut to the centre of each cookie and leave to set.

Makes about 30

* 225 g/8 oz butter, softened
* 140 g/5 oz golden caster sugar
* 1 egg yolk, lightly beaten
* 225 g/8 oz plain flour
  55 g/2 oz ground hazelnuts
* salt

To decorate
225 g/8 oz plain chocolate, broken into pieces
about 30 hazelnuts

Apricot & Pecan Cookies

1. Put the butter and sugar into a bowl and mix well with a wooden spoon, then beat in the egg yolk and vanilla extract. Sift together the flour and a pinch of salt into the mixture, add the orange rind and apricots and stir until thoroughly combined. Shape the dough into a log. Spread out the pecans in a shallow dish. Roll the log in the nuts until well coated, then wrap in clingfilm and chill in the refrigerator for 30–60 minutes.

2. Preheat the oven to 190°C/375°F/Gas Mark 5. Line 2 baking sheets with baking parchment.

3. Unwrap the dough and cut into 5-mm/¼-inch slices with a sharp serrated knife. Put the slices on the prepared baking sheets spaced well apart.

4. Bake for 10–12 minutes. Leave to cool on the baking sheets for 5–10 minutes, then using a palette knife, carefully transfer to wire racks to cool completely.

Makes about 30

* 225 g/8 oz butter, softened
* 140 g/5 oz caster sugar
* 1 egg yolk, lightly beaten
* 2 tsp vanilla extract
* 280 g/10 oz plain flour
  grated rind of 1 orange
  55 g/2 oz ready-to-eat dried apricots, chopped
  100 g/3½ oz pecan nuts, finely chopped
* salt

Pistachio & Almond Cookies

1. Put the butter and sugar into a bowl and mix well with a wooden spoon, then beat in the egg yolk and almond extract. Sift together the flour and a pinch of salt into the mixture, add the ground almonds and stir until thoroughly combined. Halve the dough, shape into balls, wrap in clingfilm and chill in the refrigerator for 30–60 minutes.

2. Preheat the oven to 190°C/375°F/Gas Mark 5. Line 2 baking sheets with baking parchment.

3. Unwrap the dough and roll out between 2 sheets of baking parchment to about 3 mm/⅛ inch thick. Sprinkle half the pistachio nuts over each piece of dough and roll lightly with the rolling pin. Stamp out cookies with a heart-shaped cutter and place on the prepared baking sheets spaced well apart.

4. Bake for 10–12 minutes. Leave to cool on the baking sheets for 5–10 minutes, then using a palette knife, carefully transfer the cookies to wire racks to cool completely.

Makes about 30

* 225 g/8 oz butter, softened
* 140 g/5 oz caster sugar
* 1 egg yolk, lightly beaten
* 2 tsp almond extract
* 225 g/8 oz plain flour
* 55 g/2 oz ground almonds
* 55 g/2 oz pistachio nuts, finely chopped
* salt

Cappuccino Cookies

1. Empty the cappuccino sachets into a small bowl and stir in the hot, but not boiling water to make a paste.

2. Put the butter and sugar into a bowl and mix well with a wooden spoon, then beat in the egg yolk and cappuccino paste. Sift together the flour and a pinch of salt into the mixture and stir until thoroughly combined. Halve the dough, shape into balls, wrap in clingfilm and chill in the refrigerator for 30–60 minutes.

3. Preheat the oven to 190°C/375°F/Gas Mark 5. Line 2 baking sheets with baking parchment.

4. Unwrap the dough and roll out between 2 sheets of baking parchment. Stamp out cookies with a 6-cm/2½-inch round cutter and put them on the prepared baking sheets spaced well apart.

5. Bake for 10–12 minutes, until golden brown. Leave to cool for 5–10 minutes, then carefully transfer to wire racks to cool completely.

6. When the cookies are cool, place the wire racks over a sheet of baking parchment. Put the chocolate into a heatproof bowl and melt over a pan of gently simmering water. Remove the bowl from the heat and leave to cool, then spoon the chocolate over the cookies. Gently tap the wire racks to level the surface and leave to set. Dust lightly with cocoa powder.

Makes about 30

2 sachets instant cappuccino

1 tbsp hot water

225 g/8 oz butter, softened

140 g/5 oz caster sugar

1 egg yolk, lightly beaten

280 g/10 oz plain flour

175 g/6 oz white chocolate, broken into pieces

salt

cocoa powder, for dusting

Cinnamon & Orange Crisps

1. Put the butter, 140 g/5 oz of the sugar and the orange rind into a bowl and mix well with a wooden spoon, then beat in the egg yolk and 2 tsp of the orange juice. Sift together the flour and a pinch of salt into the mixture, add the remaining sugar and stir until thoroughly combined. Shape the dough into a ball, wrap in clingfilm and chill for 30–60 minutes.

2. Unwrap the dough and roll out between 2 sheets of baking parchment into a 30-cm/12-inch square. Brush with the remaining orange juice and sprinkle with the cinnamon. Lightly roll with the rolling pin. Roll up the dough like a Swiss roll. Wrap in clingfilm and chill in the refrigerator for 30 minutes.

3. Preheat the oven to 190°C/375°F/Gas Mark 5. Line 2 baking sheets with baking parchment.

4. Unwrap the dough and using a sharp knife, cut into thin slices. Put them on the prepared baking sheets spaced well apart and bake for 10–12 minutes. Leave to cool on the baking sheets for 5–10 minutes, then using a palette knife, carefully transfer to wire racks to cool completely.

Makes about 30

* 225 g/8 oz butter, softened
* 200 g/7 oz caster sugar
  grated rind of 1 orange
* 1 egg yolk, lightly beaten
  4 tsp orange juice
* 280 g/10 oz plain flour
  2 tsp ground cinnamon
* salt

Party

21

Iced Stars

1. Put the butter and sugar into a bowl and mix well with a wooden spoon, then beat in the egg yolk and vanilla extract. Sift together the flour and a pinch of salt into the mixture and stir until thoroughly combined. Halve the dough, shape into balls, wrap in clingfilm and chill in the refrigerator for 30–60 minutes.

2. Preheat the oven to 190°C/375°F/Gas Mark 5. Line 2 baking sheets with baking parchment.

3. Unwrap the dough and roll out between 2 sheets of baking parchment to about 3 mm/⅛ inch thick. Stamp out cookies with a star-shaped cutter and put them on the prepared baking sheets spaced well apart.

4. Bake for 10–15 minutes, until light golden brown. Leave to cool on the baking sheets for 5–10 minutes, then using a palette knife, carefully transfer to wire racks to cool completely.

5. To decorate, sift the icing sugar into a bowl and stir in 1–2 tablespoons of warm water until the mixture has the consistency of thick cream. Divide the icing among 3–4 bowls and add a few drops of your chosen food colourings to each. Leave the cookies on the racks and spread the different coloured icings over them to the edges. Arrange silver and gold balls on top and/or sprinkle with hundreds and thousands etc. If you like, colour desiccated coconut with edible food colouring in a contrasting colour. Leave the cookies to set.

Makes about 30

- ✳ 225 g/8 oz butter, softened
- ✳ 140 g/5 oz caster sugar
- ✳ 1 egg yolk, lightly beaten
- ✳ ½ tsp vanilla extract
- ✳ 280 g/10 oz plain flour
- ✳ salt

To decorate
200 g/7 oz icing sugar
edible food colourings
silver and gold balls
hundreds and thousands
desiccated coconut
sugar sprinkles
sugar stars, hearts and flowers

Chocolate Buttons

1. Empty the chocolate drink sachets into a bowl and stir in the hot water to make a paste. Put the butter and sugar into a bowl and mix well with a wooden spoon, then beat in the egg yolk and chocolate paste. Sift together the flour and a pinch of salt into the mixture and stir until thoroughly combined. Halve the dough, shape into balls, wrap in clingfilm and chill in the refrigerator for 30–60 minutes.

2. Preheat the oven to 190°C/375°F/Gas Mark 5. Line 2 baking sheets with baking parchment.

3. Unwrap the dough and roll out between 2 sheets of baking parchment to 3 mm/⅛ inch thick. Stamp out rounds with a plain 5-cm/2-inch cutter. Using a 3-cm/1¼-inch cap from a soft drink or mineral water bottle, make an indentation in the centre of each button. Using a wooden toothpick, make 4 holes in the centre of each button, then put them on the prepared baking sheets spaced well apart. Sprinkle with caster sugar.

4. Bake for 10–15 minutes, until firm. Leave to cool on the baking sheets for 5–10 minutes, then using a palette knife, transfer to wire racks to cool completely.

Makes about 30

2 sachets instant chocolate or fudge chocolate drink

1 tbsp hot water

225 g/8 oz butter, softened

140 g/5 oz caster sugar, plus extra for sprinkling

1 egg yolk, lightly beaten

280 g/10 oz plain flour

salt

Name Cookies

1. Put the butter and sugar into a bowl and mix well with a wooden spoon, then beat in the egg yolk, orange juice or liqueur and grated rind. Sift together the flour and a pinch of salt into the mixture and stir until thoroughly combined. Halve the dough, shape into balls, wrap in clingfilm and chill in the refrigerator for 30–60 minutes.

2. Preheat the oven to 190°C/375°F/Gas Mark 5. Line 2 baking sheets with baking parchment.

3. Unwrap the dough and roll out to about 3 mm/⅛ inch thick. Depending on the occasion and age group, stamp out appropriate shapes with cookie cutters. Put the cookies on the prepared baking sheets spaced well apart.

4. Bake for 10–15 minutes, until light golden brown. Leave to cool for 5–10 minutes, then carefully transfer to wire racks to cool completely.

5. Leave the cookies on the racks. Put the egg white and icing sugar into a bowl and beat until smooth, adding a very little water if necessary (the icing should just hold its shape). Transfer half the icing to another bowl and colour each bowl of icing with a different colour.

6. Put both icings in piping bags with fine tips or into small plastic bags (see page 5). Decorate with sweets, green balls or crystallized flowers and leave to set.

Makes 25–30

* 225 g/8 oz butter, softened
* 140 g/5 oz caster sugar
* 1 egg yolk, lightly beaten
  2 tsp orange juice or orange liqueur
  grated rind of 1 orange
* 280 g/10 oz plain flour
* salt

To decorate
1 egg white
225 g/8 oz icing sugar
few drops each of 2 edible food colours
small sweets, green balls or crystallized flowers

Sugared Hearts

1. Put the butter and half the sugar into a bowl and mix well with a wooden spoon, then beat in the egg yolk and vanilla extract. Sift together the flour, cocoa powder and a pinch of salt into the mixture and stir until thoroughly combined. Halve the dough, shape into balls, wrap in clingfilm and chill in the refrigerator for 30–60 minutes.

2. Preheat the oven to 190°C/375°F/Gas Mark 5. Line 2 baking sheets with baking parchment.

3. Unwrap the dough and roll out between 2 sheets of baking parchment. Stamp out cookies with a heart-shaped cutter and put them on the prepared baking sheets spaced well apart.

4. Bake for 10–15 minutes, until firm. Leave to cool on the baking sheets for 5–10 minutes, then using a palette knife, carefully transfer to wire racks to cool completely.

5. Meanwhile, divide the remaining sugar among 4 small plastic bags or bowls. Add a little food colouring paste to each and rub in until well mixed. (Wear a plastic glove if mixing in bowls to prevent staining.) Put the chocolate in a heatproof bowl and melt over a pan of gently simmering water. Remove from the heat and leave to cool slightly.

6. Leave the cookies on the racks. Spread the melted chocolate over them and sprinkle with the coloured sugar. Leave to set.

Makes about 30

* 225 g/8 oz butter, softened
* 280 g/10 oz caster sugar
* 1 egg yolk, lightly beaten
* 2 tsp vanilla extract
* 250 g/9 oz plain flour
  25 g/1 oz cocoa powder
  3–4 food colouring pastes
  100 g/3½ oz plain chocolate, broken into pieces
* salt

Margarita Cookies

1. Preheat the oven to 190°C/375°F/Gas Mark 5. Line 2 baking sheets with baking parchment.

2. Put the butter, sugar and lime rind into a bowl and mix well with a wooden spoon, then beat in the egg yolk and orange liqueur or orange extract. Sift together the flour and a pinch of salt into the mixture and stir until thoroughly combined.

3. Scoop up tablespoons of the dough and put them on the prepared baking sheets, then flatten gently. Bake for 10–15 minutes, until light golden brown. Leave to cool on the baking sheets for 5–10 minutes, then using a palette knife, carefully transfer to wire racks to cool completely.

4. Sift the icing sugar into a bowl and stir in sufficient tequila to give the mixture the consistency of thick cream. Leave the cookies on the racks and drizzle the icing over them with a teaspoon. Leave to set.

Makes about 30

* 225 g/8 oz butter, softened
* 140 g/5 oz caster sugar
  finely grated rind of 1 lime
* 1 egg yolk, lightly beaten
  2 tsp orange liqueur or 1 tsp orange extract
* 280 g/10 oz plain flour
* salt

To decorate
140 g/5 oz icing sugar
2 tbsp white tequila

26

Caribbean Cookies

1. Preheat the oven to 190°C/375°F/Gas Mark 5. Line 2 baking sheets with baking parchment.

2. Put the butter and sugar into a bowl and mix well with a wooden spoon, then beat in the egg yolk and rum or rum flavouring. Sift together the flour and a pinch of salt into the mixture, add the coconut and stir until thoroughly combined.

3. Scoop up tablespoons of the dough and put them on the prepared baking sheets spaced well apart. Make a hollow in the centre of each with the dampened handle of a wooden spoon. Fill the hollows with lime marmalade.

4. Bake for 10–15 minutes, until light golden brown. Leave to cool on the baking sheets for 5–10 minutes, then using a palette knife, carefully transfer to wire racks to cool completely.

Makes about 30

* 225 g/8 oz butter, softened
* 140 g/5 oz caster sugar
* 1 egg yolk, lightly beaten
* 2 tsp rum or rum flavouring
* 280 g/10 oz plain flour
* 100 g/3½ oz desiccated coconut
* 4 tbsp lime marmalade
* salt

27

Easter Bunny Cookies

1. Put the butter and sugar into a bowl and mix well with a wooden spoon, then beat in the egg yolk and vanilla extract. Sift together the flour, cocoa powder and a pinch of salt into the mixture, add the ginger and stir until thoroughly combined. Halve the dough, shape into balls, wrap in clingfilm and chill in the refrigerator for 30–60 minutes.

2. Preheat the oven to 190°C/375°F/Gas Mark 5. Line 2 baking sheets with baking parchment.

3. Unwrap the dough and roll out between 2 sheets of baking parchment. Stamp out 15 rounds with a 5-cm/2-inch plain cutter (bodies), 15 rounds with a 3-cm/1¼-inch plain cutter (heads), 30 rounds with a 2-cm/¾-inch plain cutter (ears) and 15 rounds with a 1-cm/½-inch plain cutter (tails). Make up the bunnies on the baking sheets spaced well apart.

4. Bake for 7 minutes, then brush the bunnies with egg white and sprinkle with caster sugar. Return to the oven and bake for a further 5–8 minutes. Remove from the oven and put a mini marshmallow in the centre of each tail. Return to the oven for 1 minute. Leave to cool for 5–10 minutes, then carefully transfer to wire racks to cool completely.

5. Sift the icing sugar into a bowl and stir in enough water to give the icing the consistency of thick cream. Add a few drops of food colouring. Pipe a collar where the heads and bodies join and add initials if desired. Leave to set.

Makes about 15

* 225 g/8 oz butter, softened
* 140 g/5 oz caster sugar, plus extra for sprinkling
* 1 egg yolk, lightly beaten
* 2 tsp vanilla extract
* 250 g/9 oz plain flour
  25 g/1 oz cocoa powder
  2 tbsp finely chopped stem ginger
  1 egg white, lightly beaten
  15 white mini marshmallows
  140 g/5 oz icing sugar
  few drops of edible pink food colouring
* salt

68

28

Traditional Easter Cookies

1. Put the butter and sugar into a bowl and mix well with a wooden spoon, then beat in the egg yolk. Sift together the flour, mixed spice and a pinch of salt into the mixture, add the mixed peel and currants and stir until thoroughly combined. Halve the dough, shape into balls, wrap in clingfilm and chill in the refrigerator for 30–60 minutes.

2. Preheat the oven to 190°C/375°F/Gas Mark 5. Line 2 baking sheets with baking parchment.

3. Unwrap the dough and roll out between 2 sheets of baking parchment. Stamp out cookies with a 6-cm/2½-inch fluted round cutter and put them on the prepared baking sheets spaced well apart.

4. Bake for 7 minutes, then brush with the egg white and sprinkle with caster sugar. Return to the oven and bake for a further 5–8 minutes, until light golden brown. Leave to cool on the baking sheets for 5–10 minutes, then using a palette knife, carefully transfer to wire racks to cool completely.

Makes about 30

* 225 g/8 oz butter, softened
* 140 g/5 oz caster sugar, plus extra for sprinkling
* 1 egg yolk, lightly beaten
* 280 g/10 oz plain flour
  1 tsp mixed spice
  1 tbsp mixed peel
  55 g/2 oz currants
  1 egg white, lightly beaten
* salt

Christmas Angels

1. Put the butter and sugar into a bowl and mix well with a wooden spoon, then beat in the egg yolk and passion fruit pulp. Sift together the flour and a pinch of salt into the mixture, add the coconut and stir until thoroughly combined. Halve the dough, shape into balls, wrap in clingfilm and chill in the refrigerator for 30–60 minutes.

2. Preheat the oven to 190°C/375°F/Gas Mark 5. Line 2 baking sheets with baking parchment.

3. Unwrap the dough and roll out between 2 sheets of baking parchment. Stamp out cookies with a 7-cm/2¾-inch angel-shaped cutter and put them on the prepared baking sheets spaced well apart.

4. Bake for 10–15 minutes, until light golden brown. Leave to cool on the baking sheets for 5–10 minutes, then using a palette knife, carefully transfer to wire racks to cool completely.

5. Sift the icing sugar into a bowl and stir in the passion fruit pulp until the icing has the consistency of thick cream. Leave the cookies on the racks and spread the icing over them. Sprinkle with the edible glitter and leave to set.

Makes about 25

※ 225 g/8 oz butter, softened
※ 140 g/5 oz caster sugar
※ 1 egg yolk, lightly beaten
2 tsp passion fruit pulp
※ 280 g/10 oz plain flour
55 g/2 oz desiccated coconut
※ salt

To decorate
175 g/6 oz icing sugar
1–1½ tbsp passion fruit pulp
edible silver glitter, for sprinkling

Christmas Bells

1. Put the butter, sugar and lemon rind into a bowl and mix well with a wooden spoon, then beat in the egg yolk. Sift together the flour, cinnamon and a pinch of salt into the mixture, add the chocolate chips and stir until thoroughly combined. Halve the dough, shape into balls, wrap in clingfilm and chill in the refrigerator for 30–60 minutes.

2. Preheat the oven to 190°C/375°F/Gas Mark 5. Line 2 baking sheets with baking parchment.

3. Unwrap the dough and roll out between 2 sheets of baking parchment. Stamp out cookies with a 5-cm/2-inch bell-shaped cutter and put them on the prepared baking sheets spaced well apart.

4. Bake for 10–15 minutes, until light golden brown. Leave to cool on the baking sheets for 5–10 minutes, then using a palette knife, carefully transfer to wire racks to cool completely.

5. Mix together the egg white and lemon juice in a bowl, then gradually beat in the icing sugar until smooth. Leave the cookies on the racks and spread the icing over them. Place a silver ball on the clapper shape at the bottom of the cookie and leave to set completely. When the icing is dry, use the food colouring pens to draw patterns on the cookies.

Makes about 30

- 225 g/8 oz butter, softened
- 140 g/5 oz caster sugar
- finely grated rind of 1 lemon
- 1 egg yolk, lightly beaten
- 280 g/10 oz plain flour
- ½ tsp ground cinnamon
- 100 g/3½ oz plain chocolate chips
- salt

To decorate
- 2 tbsp lightly beaten egg white
- 2 tbsp lemon juice
- 225 g/8 oz icing sugar
- 30 silver balls
- food colouring pens

Fruity

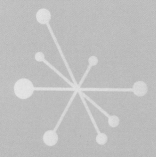

31

Pear & Pistachio Nut Cookies

1. Preheat the oven to 190°C/375°F/Gas Mark 5. Line 2 baking sheets with baking parchment.

2. Put the butter and sugar into a bowl and mix well with a wooden spoon, then beat in the egg yolk and vanilla extract. Sift together the flour and a pinch of salt into the mixture, add the pears and pistachio nuts and stir until thoroughly combined.

3. Scoop up tablespoons of the mixture and roll into balls. Put them on the prepared baking sheets spaced well apart and flatten slightly. Gently press a whole pistachio nut into the centre of each cookie.

4. Bake for 10–15 minutes, until golden brown. Leave to cool on the baking sheets for 5–10 minutes, then using a palette knife, carefully transfer to wire racks to cool completely.

Makes about 30

* 225 g/8 oz butter, softened
* 140 g/5 oz caster sugar
* 1 egg yolk, lightly beaten
* 2 tsp vanilla extract
* 280 g/10 oz plain flour
  55 g/2 oz ready-to-eat dried pears, finely chopped
  55 g/2 oz pistachio nuts, chopped
* salt
  whole pistachio nuts, to decorate

Orange & Lemon Cookies

1. Put the butter and sugar into a bowl and mix well with a wooden spoon, then beat in the egg yolk. Sift together the flour and a pinch of salt into the mixture and stir until thoroughly combined. Halve the dough and gently knead the orange rind into one half and the lemon rind into the other. Shape into balls, wrap in clingfilm and chill in the refrigerator for 30–60 minutes.

2. Preheat the oven to 190°C/375°F/Gas Mark 5. Line 2 baking sheets with baking parchment.

3. Unwrap the orange-flavoured dough and roll out between 2 sheets of baking parchment. Stamp out rounds with a 6-cm/2½-inch cutter and put them on a prepared baking sheet spaced well apart. Repeat with the lemon-flavoured dough and stamp out crescents. Put them on the other prepared baking sheet spaced well apart.

4. Bake for 10–15 minutes, until golden brown. Leave to cool for 5–10 minutes, then carefully transfer to wire racks to cool completely.

5. To decorate, mix together the egg white and lemon juice. Gradually beat in the icing sugar with a wooden spoon until smooth. Spoon half the icing into another bowl. Stir yellow food colouring into one bowl and orange into the other. Leave the cookies on the racks. Spread the icing over the cookies and decorate with the jelly slices. Leave to set.

Makes about 30

- 225 g/8 oz butter, softened
- 140 g/5 oz caster sugar
- 1 egg yolk, lightly beaten
- 280 g/10 oz plain flour
- finely grated rind of 1 orange
- finely grated rind of 1 lemon
- salt

To decorate
1 tbsp lightly beaten egg white
1 tbsp lemon juice
115 g/4 oz icing sugar
few drops yellow food colouring
few drops orange food colouring
about 15 lemon jelly slices
about 15 orange jelly slices

Banana & Raisin Cookies

1. Put the raisins into a bowl, pour in the orange juice or rum and leave to soak for 30 minutes. Drain the raisins, reserving any remaining orange juice or rum.

2. Preheat the oven to 190°C/375°F/Gas Mark 5. Line 2 baking sheets with baking parchment.

3. Put the butter and sugar into a bowl and mix well with a wooden spoon, then beat in the egg yolk and 2 teaspoons of the reserved orange juice or rum. Sift together the flour and a pinch of salt into the mixture, add the raisins and dried bananas and stir until thoroughly combined.

4. Put tablespoons of the mixture into heaps on the prepared baking sheets spaced well apart, then flatten them gently. Bake for 12–15 minutes, until golden. Leave to cool on the baking sheets for 5–10 minutes, then using a palette knife, carefully transfer to wire racks to cool completely.

Makes about 30

25 g/1 oz raisins

125 ml/4 fl oz orange juice or rum

* 225 g/8 oz butter, softened

* 140 g/5 oz caster sugar

* 1 egg yolk, lightly beaten

* 280 g/10 oz plain flour

85 g/3 oz dried bananas, finely chopped

* salt

Cherry & Chocolate Diamonds

1. Put the butter and sugar into a bowl and mix well with a wooden spoon, then beat in the egg yolk and vanilla extract. Sift together the flour and a pinch of salt into the mixture, add the glacé cherries and chocolate chips and stir until thoroughly combined. Halve the dough, shape into balls, wrap in clingfilm and chill in the refrigerator for 30–60 minutes.

2. Preheat the oven to 190°C/375°F/Gas Mark 5. Line 2 baking sheets with baking parchment.

3. Unwrap the dough and roll out between 2 sheets of baking parchment to about 3 mm/⅛ inch thick. Stamp out cookies with a diamond-shaped cutter and put them on the prepared baking sheets.

4. Bake for 10–15 minutes, until light golden brown. Leave to cool on the baking sheets for 5–10 minutes, then using a palette knife, carefully transfer to wire racks to cool completely.

Makes about 30

- 225 g/8 oz butter, softened
- 140 g/5 oz caster sugar
- 1 egg yolk, lightly beaten
- 2 tsp vanilla extract
- 280 g/10 oz plain flour
  - 55 g/2 oz glacé cherries, finely chopped
  - 55 g/2 oz milk chocolate chips
- salt

35

Grapefruit & Apple Mint Cookies

1. Put the butter and sugar into a bowl and mix well with a wooden spoon, then beat in the egg yolk and grapefruit juice. Sift together the flour and a pinch of salt into the mixture, add the grapefruit rind and chopped mint and stir until thoroughly combined. Halve the dough, shape into balls, wrap in clingfilm and chill in the refrigerator for 30–60 minutes.

2. Preheat the oven to 190°C/375°F/Gas Mark 5. Line 2 baking sheets with baking parchment.

3. Unwrap the dough and roll out between 2 sheets of baking parchment to 3 mm/⅛ inch thick. Stamp out cookies with a 5-cm/2-inch flower cutter and put them on the prepared baking sheets spaced well apart. Sprinkle with caster sugar.

4. Bake for 10–15 minutes, until golden brown. Leave to cool on the baking sheets for 5–10 minutes, then using a palette knife, carefully transfer to wire racks to cool completely.

Makes about 30

* 225 g/8 oz butter, softened
* 140 g/5 oz caster sugar, plus extra for sprinkling
* 1 egg yolk, lightly beaten
  2 tsp grapefruit juice
* 280 g/10 oz plain flour
  grated rind of 1 grapefruit
  2 tsp finely chopped fresh apple mint
* salt

36

Strawberry Pinks

1. Preheat the oven to 190°C/375°F/Gas Mark 5. Line 2 baking sheets with baking parchment.

2. Put the butter and sugar into a bowl and mix well with a wooden spoon, then beat in the egg yolk and strawberry flavouring. Sift together the flour and a pinch of salt into the mixture, add the coconut and stir until thoroughly combined.

3. Scoop up tablespoons of the mixture and roll them into balls. Put on the prepared baking sheets spaced well apart and use the handle of a wooden spoon to make a hollow in the centre of each. Fill the hollows with strawberry jam.

4. Bake for 12–15 minutes. Leave to cool on the baking sheets for 5–10 minutes, then using a palette knife, carefully transfer the cookies to wire racks to cool completely.

Makes about 30

※ 225 g/8 oz butter, softened
※ 140 g/5 oz caster sugar
※ 1 egg yolk, lightly beaten
1 tsp strawberry flavouring
※ 280 g/10 oz plain flour
100 g/3½ oz desiccated coconut
4 tbsp strawberry jam
※ salt

Coconut & Cranberry Cookies

1. Preheat the oven to 190°C/375°F/Gas Mark 5. Line 2 baking sheets with baking parchment.

2. Put the butter and sugar into a bowl and mix well with a wooden spoon, then beat in the egg yolk and vanilla extract. Sift together the flour and a pinch of salt into the mixture, add the coconut and cranberries and stir until thoroughly combined. Scoop up tablespoons of the dough and place in mounds on the prepared baking sheets spaced well apart.

3. Bake for 12–15 minutes, until golden brown. Leave to cool on the baking sheets for 5–10 minutes, then using a palette knife, carefully transfer to wire racks to cool completely.

Makes about 30

* 225 g/8 oz butter, softened
* 140 g/5 oz caster sugar
* 1 egg yolk, lightly beaten
* 2 tsp vanilla extract
* 280 g/10 oz plain flour
  40 g/1½ oz desiccated coconut
  60 g/2¼ oz dried cranberries
* salt

38

Blueberry & Orange Cookies

1. Put the butter and sugar into a bowl and mix well with a wooden spoon, then beat in the egg yolk and orange extract. Sift together the flour and a pinch of salt into the mixture, add the blueberries and stir until thoroughly combined. Shape the dough into a log, wrap in clingfilm and chill in the refrigerator for 30–60 minutes.

2. Preheat the oven to 190°C/375°F/Gas Mark 5. Line 2 baking sheets with baking parchment.

3. Unwrap the log and cut into 5-mm/¼-inch slices with a sharp serrated knife. Put them on the prepared baking sheets spaced well apart.

4. Bake for 10–15 minutes, until golden brown. Leave to cool on the baking sheets for 5–10 minutes, then using a palette knife, carefully transfer to wire racks to cool completely.

5. Just before serving, beat the cream cheese in a bowl and stir in the orange rind. Spread the mixture over the cookies and sprinkle with the chopped nuts.

Makes about 30

- 225 g/8 oz butter, softened
- 140 g/5 oz caster sugar
- 1 egg yolk, lightly beaten
- 1 tsp orange extract
- 280 g/10 oz plain flour
- 100 g/3½ oz dried blueberries
- 100 g/3½ oz cream cheese
- grated rind of 1 orange
- 40 g/1½ oz macadamia nuts, finely chopped
- salt

Oaty Raisin & Hazelnut Cookies

1. Preheat the oven to 190°C/375°F/Gas Mark 5. Line 2 baking sheets with baking parchment. Put the raisins in a bowl, add the orange juice and leave to soak for 10 minutes.

2. Put the butter and sugar into a bowl and mix well with a wooden spoon, then beat in the egg yolk and vanilla extract. Sift together the flour and a pinch of salt into the mixture and add the oats and hazelnuts. Drain the raisins, add them to the mixture and stir until thoroughly combined.

3. Scoop up tablespoons of the mixture and place them in mounds on the prepared baking sheets spaced well apart. Flatten slightly and place a whole hazelnut in the centre of each cookie.

4. Bake for 12–15 minutes, until golden brown. Leave to cool on the baking sheets for 5–10 minutes, then using a palette knife, carefully transfer the cookies to wire racks to cool completely.

Makes about 30

55 g/2 oz raisins, chopped
125 ml/4 fl oz orange juice
✳ 225 g/8 oz butter, softened
✳ 140 g/5 oz caster sugar
✳ 1 egg yolk, lightly beaten
✳ 2 tsp vanilla extract
✳ 225 g/8 oz plain flour
55 g/2 oz rolled oats
55 g/2 oz hazelnuts, chopped
✳ salt
whole hazelnuts, to decorate

Peach, Pear & Plum Cookies

1. Preheat the oven to 190°C/375°F/Gas Mark 5. Line 2 baking sheets with baking parchment.

2. Put the butter and sugar into a bowl and mix well with a wooden spoon, then beat in the egg yolk and almond extract. Sift together the flour and a pinch of salt into the mixture, add the dried fruit and stir until thoroughly combined.

3. Scoop up tablespoons of the mixture, roll them into balls and place on the prepared baking sheets spaced well apart. Make a hollow in the centre of each with the dampened handle of a wooden spoon. Fill the hollows with the jam.

4. Bake for 12–15 minutes, until light golden brown. Leave to cool on the baking sheets for 5–10 minutes, then using a palette knife, carefully transfer to wire racks to cool completely.

Makes about 30

- 225 g/8 oz butter, softened
- 140 g/5 oz caster sugar
- 1 egg yolk, lightly beaten
- 2 tsp almond extract
- 280 g/10 oz plain flour
- 55 g/2 oz ready-to-eat dried peach, finely chopped
- 55 g/2 oz ready-to-eat dried pear, finely chopped
- 4 tbsp plum jam
- salt

Double the Fun

41

Jam Rings

1. Put the butter and sugar into a bowl and mix well with a wooden spoon, then beat in the egg yolk and vanilla extract. Sift together the flour and a pinch of salt into the mixture and stir until thoroughly combined. Halve the dough, shape into balls, wrap in clingfilm and chill in the refrigerator for 30–60 minutes.

2. Preheat the oven to 190°C/375°F/Gas Mark 5. Line 2 baking sheets with baking parchment.

3. Unwrap the dough and roll out between 2 sheets of baking parchment. Stamp out cookies with a 7-cm/2¾-inch fluted round cutter and put half of them on a prepared baking sheet spaced well apart. Using a 4-cm/1½-inch plain round cutter, stamp out the centres of the remaining cookies and remove. Put the cookie rings on the other baking sheet spaced well apart.

4. Bake for 7 minutes, then brush the cookie rings with beaten egg white and sprinkle with caster sugar. Bake for a further 5–8 minutes, until light golden brown. Leave to cool on the baking sheets for 5–10 minutes, then using a palette knife, carefully transfer to wire racks to cool completely.

5. To make the jam filling, beat the butter and icing sugar together in a bowl until smooth and combined. Spread the buttercream over the whole cookies and top with a little jam. Place the cookie rings on top and press gently together.

Makes about 15

* 225 g/8 oz butter, softened
* 140 g/5 oz caster sugar, plus extra for sprinkling
* 1 egg yolk, lightly beaten
* 2 tsp vanilla extract
* 280 g/10 oz plain flour
  1 egg white, lightly beaten
* salt

Jam filling
55 g/2 oz butter, softened
100 g/3½ oz icing sugar
5 tbsp strawberry or raspberry jam

42

Mint Cookies with White Chocolate Ganache

1. Put the butter and sugar into a bowl and mix well with a wooden spoon, then beat in the egg yolk and vanilla extract. Sift together the flour and a pinch of salt into the mixture, add the chocolate and mint sticks and stir until thoroughly combined. Halve the dough, shape into balls, wrap in clingfilm and chill in the refrigerator for 30–60 minutes.

2. Preheat the oven to 190°C/375°F/Gas Mark 5. Line 2 baking sheets with baking parchment.

3. Unwrap the dough and roll out between 2 sheets of baking parchment. Stamp out cookies with a 6-cm/2½-inch fluted round cutter and put them on the prepared baking sheets spaced well apart.

4. Bake for 10–15 minutes, until light golden brown. Leave to cool on the baking sheets for 5–10 minutes, then using a palette knife, carefully transfer to wire racks to cool completely.

5. To make the white chocolate ganache, pour the cream into a pan, add the chocolate and melt over a low heat, stirring occasionally, until smooth. Remove the pan from the heat and leave to cool, then chill in the refrigerator until the mixture has a spreadable consistency.

6. Spread the ganache over half the cookies and top with the remaining cookies. Dust with sifted icing sugar.

Makes about 15

* 225 g/8 oz butter, softened
* 140 g/5 oz caster sugar
* 1 egg yolk, lightly beaten
* 2 tsp vanilla extract
* 280 g/10 oz plain flour
  100 g/3½ oz chocolate and mint sticks, finely chopped
* salt
  icing sugar, for dusting

White chocolate ganache
2 tbsp double cream
100 g/3½ oz white chocolate, broken into pieces

Rum & Raisin Cookies with Orange Filling

1. Put the raisins into a bowl, pour in the rum and leave to soak for 15 minutes, then drain, reserving any remaining rum. Preheat the oven to 190°C/375°F/Gas Mark 5. Line 2 baking sheets with baking parchment.

2. Put the butter and sugar into a bowl and mix well with a wooden spoon, then beat in the egg yolk and 2 teaspoons of the reserved rum. Sift together the flour and a pinch of salt into the mixture, add the raisins and stir until thoroughly combined.

3. Scoop up tablespoons of the dough and put them on the prepared baking sheets spaced well apart. Flatten gently and smooth the tops with the back of a spoon.

4. Bake for 10–15 minutes, until light golden brown. Leave to cool on the baking sheets for 5–10 minutes, then using a palette knife, carefully transfer to wire racks to cool completely.

5. To make the orange filling, sift the icing sugar into a bowl, add the butter, orange rind, rum and food colouring, if using, and beat well until smooth. Spread the filling over half the cookies and top with the remaining cookies.

Makes about 30

100 g/3½ oz raisins
150 ml/5 fl oz rum
225 g/8 oz butter, softened
140 g/5 oz caster sugar
1 egg yolk, lightly beaten
280 g/10 oz plain flour
salt

Orange filling
175 g/6 oz icing sugar
85 g/3 oz butter, softened
2 tsp finely grated orange rind
1 tsp rum
few drops of yellow edible food colouring (optional)

Redcurrant & Pastry Cream Cookies

1. Mix the butter and sugar, then beat in the egg yolk and vanilla extract. Sift in the flour and a pinch of salt and stir. Halve the dough, wrap and chill for 45 minutes.

2. Preheat the oven to 190°C/375°F/Gas Mark 5. Line 2 baking sheets with baking parchment.

3. Roll out the dough between the sheets of baking parchment. Stamp out cookies with a 6-cm/2½-inch cutter, put on the baking sheets and bake for 12 minutes, until golden. Cool for 5 minutes, then transfer to wire racks.

4. To make the pastry cream, beat the egg yolk and sugar. Sift in the flours and beat well. Stir in 3 tablespoons of the milk and the vanilla extract. Bring the remaining milk to the boil, then whisk it into the mixture. Return to the pan and bring to the boil, stirring. Remove from the heat and beat until cool.

5. Stiffly whisk the egg white. Spoon a little custard into a bowl, fold in the egg white, then fold into the rest of the custard. Heat for 2 minutes, stirring, then leave to cool. Meanwhile dip the bunches of redcurrants into the egg white and roll in the caster sugar. Leave to dry.

6. Sandwich pairs of cookies together with the pastry cream. Sift the icing sugar into a bowl, stir in the lemon extract and enough warm water to make a smooth icing. Spread it on the cookies and decorate with redcurrants.

Makes about 15

* 225 g/8 oz butter, softened
* 140 g/5 oz caster sugar
* 1 egg yolk, lightly beaten
* 2 tsp vanilla extract
* 280 g/10 oz plain flour
* salt

Pastry cream
2 egg yolks, lightly beaten
4 tbsp caster sugar
1 tbsp cornflour
1 heaped tbsp plain flour
300 ml/10 fl oz milk
few drops of vanilla extract
1 egg white

To decorate
15 small bunches of redcurrants
1 egg white, lightly beaten
2–3 tbsp caster sugar
225 g/8 oz icing sugar
¼ tsp lemon extract
2 tbsp warm water

Pineapple & Ginger Creams

1. Put the butter and sugar into a bowl and mix well with a wooden spoon, then beat in the egg yolk and vanilla extract. Sift together the flour and a pinch of salt into the mixture, add the pineapple and stir until thoroughly combined. Halve the dough, shape into balls, wrap in clingfilm and chill in the refrigerator for 30–60 minutes.

2. Preheat the oven to 190°C/375°F/Gas Mark 5. Line 2 baking sheets with baking parchment.

3. Unwrap the dough and roll out between 2 sheets of baking parchment. Stamp out cookies with a 6-cm/2½-inch fluted round cutter and put them on the prepared baking sheets spaced well apart.

4. Bake for 10–15 minutes, until light golden brown. Leave to cool on the baking sheets for 5–10 minutes, then using a palette knife, carefully transfer to wire racks to cool completely.

5. To make the ginger cream, beat the yogurt, syrup and ginger in a bowl until thoroughly combined. Sandwich the cookies together with the ginger cream. Cover half of each cookie with a piece of paper and dust the exposed half with sifted cocoa powder. Cover the cocoa-dusted half of each cookie with a piece of paper and dust the exposed half with sifted icing sugar.

Makes about 15

- 225 g/8 oz butter, softened
- 140 g/5 oz caster sugar
- 1 egg yolk, lightly beaten
- 2 tsp vanilla extract
- 280 g/10 oz plain flour
- 100 g/3½ oz ready-to-eat dried pineapple, finely chopped
- salt
- cocoa powder, for dusting
- icing sugar, for dusting

Ginger cream
- 150 ml/5 fl oz Greek-style yogurt
- 1 tbsp golden syrup
- 1 tbsp ground ginger

Crunchy Nut & Honey Sandwich Cookies

1. Preheat the oven to 190°C/375°F/Gas Mark 5. Line 2 baking sheets with baking parchment.

2. Put 225 g/8 oz of the butter and the caster sugar into a bowl and mix well with a wooden spoon, then beat in the egg yolk and vanilla extract. Sift together the flour and a pinch of salt into the mixture and stir until thoroughly combined.

3. Scoop up tablespoons of the dough and roll into balls. Put half of them on a prepared baking sheet spaced well apart and flatten gently. Spread out the nuts in a shallow dish and dip one side of the remaining dough balls into them, then place on the other baking sheet, nut side uppermost, and flatten gently.

4. Bake for 10–15 minutes, until light golden brown. Leave to cool on the baking sheets for 5–10 minutes, then using a palette knife, carefully transfer to wire racks to cool completely.

5. Beat the remaining butter with the icing sugar and honey until creamy and thoroughly mixed. Spread the honey mixture over the plain cookies and top with the nut-coated cookies.

Makes about 30

* 300 g/10½ oz butter, softened
* 140 g/5 oz caster sugar
* 1 egg yolk, lightly beaten
* 2 tsp vanilla extract
* 280 g/10 oz plain flour
* 40 g/1½ oz macadamia nuts, cashew nuts or pine kernels, chopped
* 85 g/3 oz icing sugar
* 85 g/3 oz clover or other set honey
* salt

Chocolate & Orange Cookie Sandwiches

1. Preheat the oven to 190°C/375°F/Gas Mark 5. Line 2 baking sheets with baking parchment.

2. Put the butter, sugar and orange rind into a bowl and mix well with a wooden spoon, then beat in the egg yolk and vanilla extract. Sift together the flour, cocoa powder and a pinch of salt into the mixture, add the chopped chocolate and stir until thoroughly combined.

3. Scoop up tablespoons of the dough, roll into balls and place on the prepared baking sheets spaced well apart. Gently flatten and smooth the tops with the back of a spoon.

4. Bake for 10–15 minutes, until light golden brown. Leave to cool on the baking sheets for 5–10 minutes, then using a palette knife, carefully transfer to wire racks to cool completely.

5. To make the chocolate filling, bring the cream to the boil in a small saucepan, then remove the pan from the heat. Stir in the chocolate until the mixture is smooth, then stir in the orange extract. When the mixture is completely cool, use to sandwich the cookies together in pairs.

Makes about 15

* 225 g/8 oz butter, softened
* 140 g/5 oz caster sugar
* 2 tsp finely grated orange rind
* 1 egg yolk, lightly beaten
* 2 tsp vanilla extract
* 250 g/9 oz plain flour
* 25 g/1 oz cocoa powder
* 100 g/3½ oz plain chocolate, finely chopped
* salt

Chocolate filling
125 ml/4 fl oz double cream
200 g/7 oz white chocolate, broken into pieces
1 tsp orange extract

48

Marshmallow S'mores

1. Put the butter, sugar and orange rind into a bowl and mix well with a wooden spoon, then beat in the egg yolk. Sift together the flour, cocoa powder, cinnamon and a pinch of salt into the mixture and stir until thoroughly combined. Halve the dough, shape into balls, wrap in clingfilm and chill in the refrigerator for 30–60 minutes.

2. Preheat the oven to 190°C/375°F/Gas Mark 5. Line 2 baking sheets with baking parchment.

3. Unwrap the dough and roll out between 2 sheets of baking parchment. Stamp out cookies with a 6-cm/2½-inch fluted round cutter and put them on the prepared baking sheets spaced well apart.

4. Bake for 10–15 minutes. Leave to cool for 5 minutes. Turn half the cookies upside down and put 4 marshmallow halves on each. Return to the oven and cook for 1–2 minutes. Transfer the cookies to wire racks and leave to stand for 30 minutes.

5. Melt the chocolate in a heatproof bowl set over a pan of gently simmering water. Remove from the heat and leave to cool. Line a tray or baking sheet with baking parchment. Spread the marmalade over the undersides of the uncovered cookies and place them on top of the marshmallow-covered cookies. Dip the cookies in the melted chocolate to coat, letting the excess drip back into the bowl, then place them on the tray or baking sheet. Put a walnut half in the centre of each cookie. Leave to set.

Makes about 15

- 225 g/8 oz butter, softened
- 140 g/5 oz caster sugar
- 2 tsp finely grated orange rind
- 1 egg yolk, lightly beaten
- 250 g/9 oz plain flour
- 25 g/1 oz cocoa powder
- ½ tsp ground cinnamon
- 30 yellow marshmallows, halved horizontally
- 300 g/10½ oz dark chocolate, broken into pieces
- 4 tbsp orange marmalade
- 15 walnut halves
- salt

49

Tropical Fruit & Mascarpone Cream Cookie Sandwiches

1. Put the butter and sugar into a bowl and mix well with a wooden spoon, then beat in the egg yolk and passion fruit pulp. Sift together the flour and a pinch of salt into the mixture, add the mango, papaya and dates and stir until thoroughly combined. Shape the dough into a log, wrap in clingfilm and chill in the refrigerator for 30–60 minutes.

2. Meanwhile, make the mascarpone cream. Put all the ingredients in a bowl and beat with a wooden spoon until thoroughly combined and smooth. Cover the bowl with clingfilm and chill in the refrigerator.

3. Preheat the oven to 190°C/375°F/Gas Mark 5. Line 2 baking sheets with baking parchment.

4. Unwrap the dough and cut into slices with a sharp serrated knife. Put them on the prepared baking sheets spaced well apart.

5. Bake for 10–15 minutes, until light golden brown. Leave to cool on the baking sheets for 5–10 minutes, then using a palette knife, carefully transfer to wire racks to cool completely. When the cookies are cold spread the chilled mascarpone cream over half of them, sprinkle with the toasted coconut and top with the remaining cookies.

Makes about 15

- 225 g/8 oz butter, softened
- 140 g/5 oz caster sugar
- 1 egg yolk, lightly beaten
- 2 tsp passion fruit pulp
- 280 g/10 oz plain flour
- 40 g/1½ oz ready-to-eat dried mango, chopped
- 40 g/1½ oz ready-to-eat dried papaya, chopped
- 25 g/1 oz dried dates, stoned and chopped
- 3–4 tbsp shredded coconut, toasted
- salt

Mascarpone cream
85 g/3 oz mascarpone cheese
3 tbsp Greek-style yogurt
7 tbsp ready-made custard
½ tsp ground ginger

Ice Cream Cookie Sandwiches

1. Put the butter and sugar into a bowl and mix well with a wooden spoon, then beat in the egg yolk, ginger and ginger syrup. Sift together the flour, cocoa powder, cinnamon and a pinch of salt into the mixture and stir until thoroughly combined. Halve the dough, shape into balls, wrap in clingfilm and chill in the refrigerator for 30–60 minutes.

2. Preheat the oven to 190°C/375°F/Gas Mark 5. Line 2 baking sheets with baking parchment.

3. Unwrap the dough and roll out between 2 sheets of baking parchment. Stamp out cookies with a 6-cm/2½-inch fluted round cutter and put them on the prepared baking sheets spaced well apart.

4. Bake for 10–15 minutes, until light golden brown. Leave to cool on the baking sheets for 5–10 minutes, then using a palette knife, carefully transfer to wire racks to cool completely.

5. Remove the ice cream from the freezer about 15 minutes before serving to allow it to soften. Put a generous scoop of ice cream on half the cookies and top with the remaining cookies. Press together gently so that the filling spreads to the edges. If not serving immediately, wrap the cookies individually in foil and store in the freezer.

Makes about 30

- 225 g/8 oz butter, softened
- 140 g/5 oz golden caster sugar
- 1 egg yolk, lightly beaten
- 2 tbsp finely chopped stem ginger, plus 2 tsp syrup from the jar
- 250 g/9 oz plain flour
- 25 g/1 oz cocoa powder
- ½ tsp ground cinnamon
- 450 ml/15 fl oz vanilla, chocolate or coffee ice cream
- salt